When Athletes Pray

Samantha Pegues, Hiram Wadlington,

CJ Terrell, Jeremiah Pegues,

and Jarkel Joiner

Dedication

This book is dedicated to: Xavian Herod, Samuel Woodall, Madisyn Herron, Erika Sisk, Emonica Booker, Caliya Toles, Briunna Ducksworth, Tiara King, KJ Wadley, Derrian Pegues, Gregory Milliner, Luther Hayes, Devin Rockette, Marea Burt, D'Erica Booker, Martice Rucker, Vallerie Coleman, Dontarius Thompson, Shelby McEwen, Dekaylin Metcalf, Daisa Alexander, Jaidyn Young, Jada Steen, Jahmal Pegues, Joshua Dennis, Jalen Southern, Kimaya Dixon, Shaniya Buford, Azariah Buford, Kemariaha White, Terry Williams, Drew Bianco, Ben Bianco, Matthew Toles, Jamie Shaw Jr., Brandon Turnage, DK Buford, Jacrisciah Thornton, Jameel Thompson, Jada Jones, Demetrius Barnes, Desmond Barnes, Chelsea Allen, Kemari Kinds, Orianna Shaw, Jeremi Woodall, Cemiah McGee, Zharia Mecalf, Caleb Carruthers, Jakyus Woodall, Brandeis Pettis, Keuntae Booker, Xxavier Hill, Sa'Maria Jones, Jaidyn Young, LaMarcus Faulkner, Ky Egerson, Alexus Malone, Alexus Weekly, Hailey Meeks, Haidyn Meeks, Emory Pitts, Harkievous Meeks, and Christian Blake.

Contents

Keep It Moving

As a Point Guard, sometimes I would dribble the ball down the court, pass it, and stand there to see if my teammates were going to score. My coach would yell, "What are you doing? Why are you just standing there? You have to move even when you don't have the ball in your hands!" I was thinking, "I'm standing here because I'm tired. Don't you see me sweating and breathing hard?" However, out of respect for my coach, I never talked back to him. Instead, I would suck it up and move even though I didn't have the ball. As result, I would often find myself in position to score.

Don't have the money to go to college? Apply anyway. Maybe you're at a standstill because you're tired of applying for jobs; only to be turned down. Don't stop! Don't just stand there and watch others fulfill their dreams! You must make moves even when you're tired and have nothing in your hands. When you move in faith, God will always set you up to score.

Prayer: Father God, you are best Coach. Thank you for pushing me when I wanted to give up and quit. Forgive me for allowing fear to cause me to be stuck at a standstill. From this day forward, I will walk by faith and not by sight; believing that you are setting me up to score. Amen.

Scripture: "Even youths will become weak and tired, and young men will fall in exhaustion. But those who trust in the Lord will find new strength. They will soar high on wings like eagles. They will run and not grow weary. They will walk and not faint." - Isaiah 40:30-31, NLT

Patience Is the Key

Have you ever felt like all of your hard work in practicing a sport was all in vain? You worked really hard day in and day out, but you still were not given the opportunity to showcase your talent. Well, that was me. I felt like I had given it my all at practices and in the weight room. I began to doubt myself. My family helped me realize that I wasn't working enough off the field or in school. I wasn't using my time wisely, putting enough trust in my faith, and I had my priorities in the wrong order.

I started praying a lot more and asking God for guidance. He led me to a different state of mind. I was able to become more fo-cused with a new outlook of understanding the real meaning of being a student athlete. As the season went on, the coaches started to see an improvement in my performance. Then, I start-ed getting more playing time. It took patience, endurance, and faith in God to gain a better outcome of the whole situation. I realized that nothing happens in my time. My plan was not God's plan. Always keep faith in God daily; not just when situ-ations are not in your favor. Pray and trust that he will handle it. When you feel like you've done all you can, turn to prayer. God will guide you into the right direction. He will never lead you down the wrong path. Just be patient. God has a plan just for you. I put my trust in God, will you?

Prayer: God, I come to you asking for forgiveness for all my sins. Thank you for everything that you've done in my life and for having so much patience with me. Continue to strengthen me in every area of my life. Teach my teammates, coaches and me how to love and have patience with each other. Allow us to motivate ourselves in your name. Amen

Scripture: "For I know the plans I have for you," says the Lord. "They are plans for good and not for disaster, to give you a future and a hope." -Jeremiah 29:11, NLT

Don't Swing at Everything

I was a terrible baseball player. I could catch well, run fast, and hit the ball extremely far. However, I didn't have the mindset of a baseball player. I would often strike out by swinging at bad pitches. I despised the thought of having to walk to first base. It made me feel like a failure and as if I was a weak person. Therefore, I swung at bad pitches that I should have walked away from.

Baseball reminds us that we shouldn't swing at everything that is thrown at us. You must grow into a place of maturity where you can stand still and not be moved by the adversity that comes your way. Just because alcohol and drugs are offered to you, that doesn't mean that you should take a hit. Guys, just because a woman throws her body at you, that doesn't mean that you should swing at it. Curves (curve balls) can be very tricky. Don't strike out! Wait for a good pitch! If you want to make it to the next level in life, you will sometimes have to walk away.

Prayer: Dear God, you are the best Umpire. Please give me discernment to correctly judge people's motives. Teach me how to be patient and wait for the opportunities that are best for me. Help me to understand that walking away from negative situations is a sign of strength; not weakness. Amen.

Scripture: "Be still in the presence of the Lord, and wait patiently for him to act. Don't worry about evil people who prosper or fret about their wicked schemes."- Psalm 37:7, NLT

When Home Feels Like You're on the Road

Most teams win more games at home than on the road. Many believe that it's because players feel the support from their family, friends and fans. Your home should be a place of comfort, love and safety. However, that is not always the case. Your family may have split up because of a divorce or death in the family. However, if you're reading this message, you are still alive, which means that you can live through your problems. Maybe you had a rough childhood and your family and friends weren't always there for you? You may have a parent who's on drugs or in jail; and the people closest to you, who should be cheering for you, are speaking against you and hoping that you fail? It's okay! Focus! You have to block out all of the noise (negativity, haters) and make the shot (reach your goal). God doesn't always give us home-court advantage. But, he still expects us to win. God has given us the power to dominate on and off the court.

Prayer: Dear God, you are so awesome. Thank you for my family, friends and enemies. Teach me how to win in negative environments. God, help me to realize that you are the real MVP. With you on my team, I'm able to win at home and on the raod. Amen.

Scripture: "What, then, shall we say in response to these things? If God is for us, who can be against us?" - Romans 8:31, NIV

Trust Your Spotter

Weight lifters often have a spotter during weight training. A spotter is a person who supports the weight lifter. The spotters' support allows weight lifters to lift more than they could normally lift safely. Each repetition gets harder as the weight lifters' muscles become tired. Consequently, they feel weaker even though they're building strength. A spotter must know when to intervene to prevent the lifter from getting hurt. When spotters see the lifters struggling, they encourage them to keep pushing and they help them to safely return the weights to the rack.

Did you know that God is the best Spotter? Sometimes, he allows us to carry a heavy weight to make our spirit stronger. It's not always easy to carry life's weight. You may feel as if your trials are repetitious. You overcome one obstacle only to be faced with another one. At times, you may feel weaker; but in time, you will realize that you're actually getting stronger. When our problems seem too difficult to bear. We must have confidence in knowing that God is always there to help us. He knows exactly when to step in to take the weight off of us. Don't ever give up on life. Keep pushing!

Prayer: Father God, you are so powerful. You are my strength when I am weak. Help me to understand that trials don't come to tear me down; they come to make me strong. Teach me how to rely on you when I feel as if I cannot make it through the day. Amen.

Scripture: "Don't be afraid, for I am with you. Don't be discouraged, for I am your God. I will strengthen you and help you. I will hold you up with my victorious right hand."-Isaiah 41:10, NLT

When Athletes Pray

When I pray, I have faith that God will help me overcome whatever I face. Praying energizes me and builds up my spirit and confidence. There are many questions that cross my mind when I'm on the field. Like, "What kind of obstacles will I face?" "Will I be able to follow the path that the plays dictate?" "Can I break through the defensive line?" Plotting a course in the game is much like life. God has set us on a course that leads us back to him if we follow his Word. When I'm playing, my mind tells me that the prize is just ahead of me. Therefore, I don't worry about who is coming after me because I'm focused on the prize. When my opponents are trying to tackle me, I continue to move forward despite how many players are trying to bring me down. I press on until I break through the defense. If I'm tackled, I run even harder on the next play.

When athletes pray, God regulates their minds. I believe that because I pray and ask for guidance, it is God who gives me strength and direction when I'm running the ball. He orders my steps. With perseverance and prayer, I'm able to penetrate the toughest defense.

Prayer: God, you are the best Full Back. Thank you for blocking my enemies. Keep me humble and give me wisdom to know that I am helpless unless I follow your lead. Order my steps according to yours. Amen

Scripture: "Brethren, I count not myself to have apprehended: but this one thing I do, forgetting those things which are behind, and reaching forth unto those things which are before, I press toward the mark for the prize of the high calling of God in Christ Jesus."- Philippians 3:13-14, KJV

Speak Life

Cheerleading is such an important sport. Cheerleaders cheer for and encourage their team throughout the game. It doesn't matter if their team is losing, they still speak positive words. They never speak negativity to their players. After a loss, cheerleaders encourage the players to keep their heads up and look forward to the next game.

Life can take you through many ups and down. One minute, it may seem as if you're winning; only to feel as if you're losing at life the next minute. You must learn to treat the bad times the same as the good times by speaking positivity over your situation. Surround yourself with friends and family who will encourage and motivate you during the hard times. Suicide is at an all-time high because there aren't enough people speaking positive confessions. Therefore, people feel as if their game (life) is over. Words are so powerful. You will have what you speak. Speak life! You are awesome and amazing! You are beautiful! You are handsome! You are intelligent and successful! Don't give up! Your best days are ahead of you!

Prayer: Dear God, you are the giver of life. Thank you for

allowing me to see another day. Teach me how to be thankful for each day that I'm given. From this day forward, your praise will forever be on my lips. Amen

Scripture: "The tongue has the power of life and death, and those who love it will eat its fruit."-Psalm 18:21, NIV

Huddle Up

Before the game, coaches and players gather together to discuss the game plan and to encourage each other. Some teams pray together to ask for protection and success. When a team is down or the game isn't going as planned, players will often take the initiative to huddle up in the middle of the game to develop another strategy and encourage their teammates. I've never heard another player gossip about anyone during a huddle.

In life, it's important to surround yourself with people who will pray for you; not just cheer you on. You need people who can see where you've gotten off track and help you develop another strategy without condemning you. It's important to pray strategic prayers. "Huddle up," simply means "be prayerful." We need encouragement and prayers ; not gossip and condemnation.

Prayer: Dear God, you are my biggest Supporter. Thank you for loving me enough to want to spend time with me. Forgive me for not spending enough time with you. Teach me how to put you first and help me develop time-management skills so that I will have more time to huddle up with you. Amen.

Scripture: "…The earnest prayer of a righteous person has great power and produces wonderful results."-James 5:16, NLT

Pace Yourself

Cross country runners have a different mindset than sprinters. They must focus on pace more than speed. Just because a person can run faster than you, that doesn't mean that they can run longer than you.

Ever been driving or riding down the street and saw a person in another vehicle speed pass you? However, you met the same person at a stop light and you passed them further down the road. It's important to not be distracted by people who you feel have reached certain land marks before you. Stop getting jealous of people who seem to be passing you; getting married, having children, getting a job, or buying a house before you. While they may be obtaining certain things before you, they may also lose them before you.

In this human race, God has us all on a different pace. Never try to live according to another person's speed. Live at your own pace. Longevity is more important than swiftness.

Prayer: Dear God, you know my end from the beginning. Thank you for leading me down the right path. Help me to live at your pace and give me perseverance and grace to finish this race. Amen.

Scripture: "...The fastest runner doesn't always win the race, and the strongest warrior doesn't always win the battle. The wise sometimes go hungry, and the skillful are not necessarily wealthy. And those who are educated don't always lead successful lives. It is all decided by chance, by being in the right place at the right time."-Ecclesiastes 9:11, NLT

Are You There Yet

It's not always the quarterback's responsibility to pass the football directly to the receiver. Sometimes the play calls for the quarterback to throw the ball to a specific location. It's the receiver's job to fight through the defense to get to the place where they can catch the ball.

Did you know that God is the best Quarterback? He is always releasing blessings, peace, joy and provision at a record-breaking speed. However, some of us don't always receive these things because we think that everything should be handed to us, instead of fighting through the opposition to get to the place to receive what God has for us. Others don't receive God's provisions because they're too lazy or fearful to move to the place where God has directed them to go so that they can be prosperous. Sometimes, we're miserable because we're out of God's will—by being in the wrong city, at the wrong job or in a relationship with the wrong person. And we often ask, "God, where are you?" However, God is not the problem; we are. God wants to richly bless us and give us things greater than our heart has the capability to desire. But, first he wants to know, "Are you there yet?" Are your heart, mind and motives in the right place? Get there!

Prayer: Dear God, you are the greatest Quarterback. Everything I need is in your hands. Forgive me for running my own route and not sticking to your game plan. Help me to fight past the fear, lust, hurt and temptation so I can receive what you have for me. Amen.

Scripture: "The LORD directs the steps of the godly. He delights in every detail of their lives."-Psalm 37:23, NLT

Be Prepared

Sports can be very fun and exciting. However, they can also be an extremely dangerous if the players aren't attentive to their surroundings.

Many times, we ask God for things that we aren't ready to receive. For example, receiving an executive level job can be harmful to your health if you aren't mentally prepared to handle the stress that comes along with it. Excelling in sports can cause you more harm than good if you aren't spiritually prepared to resist the temptations that are associated with living that lifestyle. Many phenomenal athletes cannot handle the lust, over-spending, criticism or the over expectation to achieve that they encounter. As result, many of their relationships are destroyed and they turn to drugs or alcohol. Not only do you have to be physically prepared to have a successful career in sports; you must also be prepared mentally and spiritually. Otherwise, the career that was meant to be a blessing will seem like a curse.

Prayer: Dear God, you are the best Life Coach. Forgive me for not following your advice. Thank you for not always giving me what I pray for. Help me to reach the maturity level that's necessary to properly handle what you have for me. Amen.

Scripture: "Keep alert at all times. And pray that you might be strong enough to escape these coming horrors and stand before the Son of Man."-Luke 12:36, NLT

Stay in Your Lane

When running the hundred-meter dash, you must run inside your lane. Crossing into another person's lane will cause you to be disqualified from the race.

Often times, we struggle or don't reach our full potential because we cross over into someone else's lane by trying to mimic their style of play or lifestyle. We will never win by living outside of our financial means, dating another person's spouse, or by trying to be someone who God hasn't called us to be. We aren't qualified to live someone else's dream; not even our parents' dream for our lives. Trying to function outside of the will of God will always end in a disaster. Stay on track.

Prayer: God, thank you for my life. Forgive me for trying to be like other people. Help me to be confident in who I am and thankful for the things and the people who you've placed in my life. Teach me to be grateful for what you've given me and to not covet things that other people have. Amen.

Scripture: "Many are the plans in the mind of a man, but it is the purpose of the LORD that will stand."-Proverbs 19:21, ESV

Don't Dwell on the Past

No one is perfect. In life, we will all make mistakes. We must learn from them; not dwell on them. We will make mistakes in our relationships and careers. However, if we want to be successful, we must quickly let them go and move forward.

Did you make a bad play? Maybe you struck out, got your shot blocked or received an unforced error. Your bad play may have cost your team the game. However, you can't worry about it. You must learn from your mistakes and quickly move on. God develops our character more in our failures than in our successes. It's imperative to have good character after a loss. Your team may have the lowest score at the end of the game but if you display integrity afterwards, you're still a winner. When God calls you to the sports industry, it's not about the money or fame. It's not even about winning. It's about character and giving God the glory. God will often send you through highs and extreme lows to keep you humble and dependent on him.

Prayer: Dear God, my life is in your hands. Thank you for forgiving me for the mistakes that I've made. Teach me how to develop and grow as a person so that I don't repeat the same mistakes. Help me to understand that I represent you at all times. Show me how to display good character in positive and negative situations. Amen.

Scripture: "Do not remember the things that have happened before. Do not think about the things of the past. See, I will do a new thing. It will begin happening now…"-Isaiah 43:18-19, NLT

Use Your Timeouts

Coaches call timeouts for various reasons. They sometimes call timeouts to change the game plan or to simply allow their players to rest. Players may call a timeout to prevent turning the ball over to the other team.

On the seventh day after creating the world, God called a timeout to rest. When we're focused on a goal, sometimes we don't stop to take a break. It's easy to become so engulfed with obtaining money or success that we forget to rest. There is no need to stress out or keep trying to force relationships or plans that are damaging to us. Take some time out to re-evaluate your game plan. If you want to keep your sanity and health, you must to use your timeouts. If God took time out to rest, so should we.

Prayer: Dear God, thank you for giving me the desire to be successful. Show me the game plan that you have for my life and help me to follow it. Teach me how to work hard while I rest in you. Thank you for giving me perfect physical, spiritual and mental health. Amen.

Scripture: "The LORD replied, "I will personally go with you, Moses, and I will give you rest—everything will be fine for you."-Exodus 33:14, NLT

Run!

When the quarterback hands the running back the ball, the only thing on his mind is running into the end zone. He doesn't stop to complain about how hard he's getting hit. Neither does he stop to address, curse out or fight his opponents because he knows it will slow him down.

Sometimes we're delayed or we never reach our goals (the end zone because we feel as if we must stop to address the lies, gossip and criticism from the people around us. When God gives you a vision, your only task is to run with it. Your enemies—even your friends and family may not understand because you won't always have time to stop and hang out with them. They may begin to talk about you in efforts to bring you down because they see that you're running too fast for them to keep up. Do not stop to explain yourself or argue with them. Smile at them and keep running. The only way that you should address your enemies is by dancing in the end zone.

Prayer: God, thank you for the vision that you've given me. Teach me how to focus on you more than I focus on my enemies. Help me to understand that the only way that they can bring me down is if I stoop to their level. I promise to run with your vision and guard it to the best of my ability. Amen.

Scripture: "And the Lord answered me: "Write the vision; make it plain on tablets, so that he may run who reads it."-Habakkuk 2:2, ESV

Get Your Head in the Game

Although it may not seem like it, sports require just as much mental toughness as physical ability. Your brain controls your body. Your opponents may be less skilled than you. But, if they can get into your head, they can negatively affect your game.

While it's important to have emotions, we must not be controlled by them. A person who is totally driven by their emotions is very unstable. You must learn to develop spiritual and mental toughness to handle life's oppositions, and block out the pettiness, negativity and condemnation from critics. Otherwise, you may have an emotional outburst that could cost you an important relationship and your career. It's important to always pray before, during and after the game. It will help you to build a resistance to outside distractions that come to attack your mind. Stay focused on God. Keep your head in the game.

Prayer: Dear God, you are a mind regulator. Forgive me for allowing distractions to take my mind off you. Strengthen my spirit and my mind so that I'm not easily offended. Teach me how to return love for hate. Make me deaf to the criticism from outsiders. Amen.

Scripture: "You keep him in perfect peace whose mind is stayed on you, because he trusts in you."-Isaiah 26:3, NLT

It's Not Just a Game. It's a Calling

Being an athlete is very hard in today's society. There are so many temptations that can cause you to stray you away from making the right choices. For me, basketball was my way of escape. My love for the game caused me to discipline my body and my mind and focus on what God placed in my heart. I believe that God call me to play basketball and to spread his word. In my opinion, being on the court is equivalent to a pastor preaching from the pulpit. When you're called into the sports industry, it becomes your ministry. Athletes can spread God's word to people whom the local church would never be able to reach. Parents must be careful when trying to force their children to only operate inside of a local church. God could be calling them be calling them elsewhere.

Education is also important. Your study time is just as important as the time that is spent practicing. Many athletes' careers come to an end by the age of forty. You must have something to fall back on to survive.

Prayer: Dear God, thank you for choosing me to be your representative. Forgive me not always representing you to the best of my ability. Help me develop resistance to temptation.

Teach me how to block out the things and people who come to take my focus off of you. When I am tempted to act of anger, quickly show me a way of escape. Amen.

Scripture: "I discipline my body like an athlete, training it to do what it should. Otherwise, I fear that after preaching to others, I myself might be disqualified."-1 Corinthians 9:27, NLT

Discipline

Sports teach athletes how to develop discipline. Athletes must work out to develop and maintain their speed and strength. They must also take care of their bodies by eating healthy foods and drinking plenty of water. Just as corporate professionals wake up early, get dressed and prepare for work. Athletes should do the same. Corporate professionals don't quit their jobs just because they have a bad day at work. Athletes must become disciplined enough to keep playing during rough seasons when their career isn't going as planned. Just as business professionals work hard to receive a job promotion; athletes must also work hard to earn playing time.

Positive personal skills and good work ethics are very significant to athletes. Having a good attitude is a major component to being a successful athlete. You must be able to get along with your teammates and coaches. Players, who cannot work well with others, become a hindrance to the team. Personal conflicts should never reach the arena during practice or a game. Your teammates are your protectors; not your enemies.

Prayer: Dear God, thank you for life, health and strength. Forgive me for not always taking good care of my body. Guide me on how to work well with my teammates. Teach us how to quickly resolve our conflicts without holding a grudge. Help us to remember that we are not just a team; we are a family. Amen.

Scripture: "Count it all joy, my brothers, when you meet trials of various kinds, for you know that the testing of your faith produces steadfastness. And let steadfastness have its full effect, that you may be perfect and complete, lacking nothing."-James 1:2. ESV

Get Back in the Game

When basketball players accumulate two or more fouls before half-time, the coach normally makes them sit on the bench to prevent them from fouling out. During this time, it's important for players to stay focused on the game and not be discouraged by the opposing team and fans' negative comments.

Don't let past mistakes and people's opinions of you, stop you from pursuing your dreams. Just when people think that you've fouled out, God will put you back in the game. Get off of the bench! You still have time to play! Maybe you've dropped out of school? It's okay! Get your GED and go to college or work. Maybe you've experienced a divorce or many failed relationships? No worries! You may have to sit on the bench for a while to heal. But, you still have time to find true love. You have not fouled out! Get back in the game!

Prayer: God, you know me better than I know myself. When you make me wait before answering my prayers, help me to understand that it's my time to be still and re-evaluate my actions and learn from my mistakes. Thank you for never giving up on me. Because of your grace and mercy, I have another chance to win at life. Amen.

www.ingramcontent.com/pod-product-compliance
Lightning Source LLC
Chambersburg PA
CBHW032134050726
47590CB00008B/3085